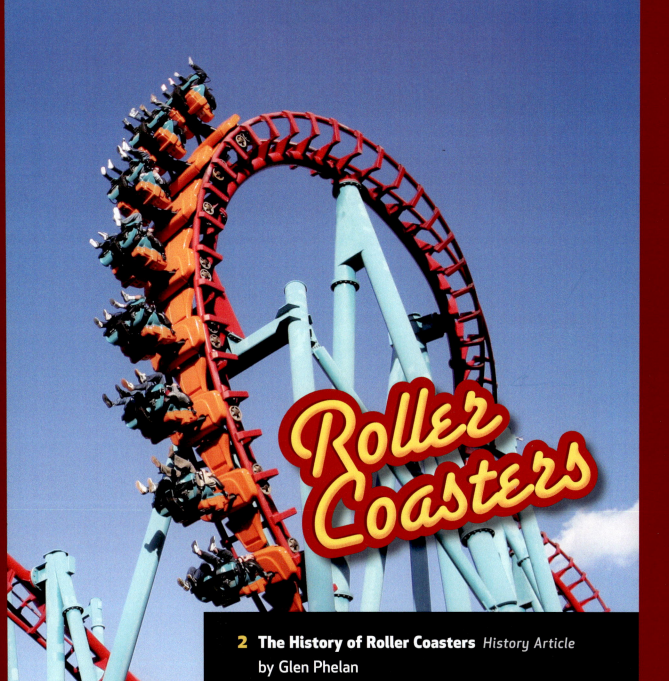

# Roller Coasters

**2** **The History of Roller Coasters** *History Article*
by Glen Phelan

**10** **Wild Coasters** *Science Article*
by Kathleen F. Lally

**18** **How to Make a Model Roller Coaster** *How-To Article*
by Judy Elgin Jensen

**24** **Discuss**

GENRE History Article   **Read to find out** how gravity plays a role in roller coaster thrills.

# THE HISTORY OF ROLLER COASTERS

by Glen Phelan

*Clack, clack, clack . . . .* The chain slowly pulls the cars up the big hill. You turn to your friend and smile. It's your first roller coaster ride. You hold the safety bar tight. Only a few more seconds to the top. *Clack, clack . . . .* Hold on!

VOOM! The cars race down the hill. Riders scream. Wheels screech. You squeeze the safety bar hard. You twist. You turn. You climb. You think you can't take one more loop-the-loop. Then the cars slow down and stop. You are back where you started.

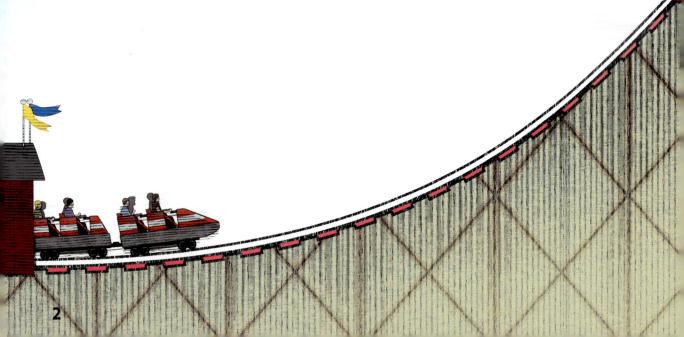

You and your friend look at each other. You both say, "Let's go again!"

Roller coasters are thrilling. But they used to be very different. The first roller coasters had no steel. They were made of wood.

### 1873

The Much Chunk Switchback Railway in Pennsylvania stops carrying coal. It starts carrying tourists up and down two mountains. Steam engines pull the cars uphill. **Gravity** pulls the cars downhill. Gravity is a **force** that pulls things toward the center of Earth. A brake controls speed while the cars coast down. The ride covers 29 kilometers (18 miles). It takes 80 minutes.

### 1817

The French build a ride with cars made from boards on wheels. The cars traveled on tracks. Axles reach from the wheels into grooves inside the tracks. This locks the wheels to the tracks. Riders roll down a curved ramp and partly up another ramp. Workers push the cars the rest of the way up. Later, cables pull the cars back up. That way riders can ride again without climbing stairs.

### 1885

The Serpentine Railway at Coney Island uses one oval track. The ride starts and ends in the same place. Riders do not get out of the car. It can go twice as fast as the Switchback Railway.

### 1887

The first figure-eight rolling ride opens in Haverhill, Massachusetts. It is in a building above an ice skating rink. Hundreds of rollers make up the track. So it is called a *roller coaster*.

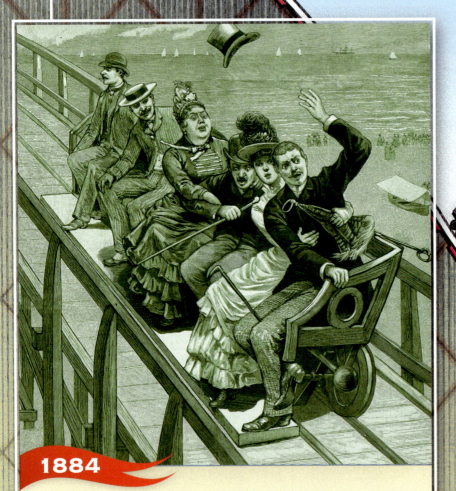

### 1884

The Switchback Railway opens at Coney Island. That's an amusement park in New York City. The car rides down and up a wavy hill. At the end of the track, the car is switched to another track. It takes the passengers back. It only goes about 10 kilometers per hour (6 miles per hour).

### 1907
Drop-the-Dips at Coney Island becomes the first roller coaster to use a lap bar for safety.

### 1910
The Venice Scenic Railway opens in Venice, California. Cars ride through tunnels. Riders can see structures and scenes from history.

### 1901
The Loop-the-Loop at Coney Island becomes the first roller coaster with a safe loop. The loops on earlier coasters were too small. Passengers were whipped around. This hurt their necks.

### 1902
Leap-the-Dips opens at Lakemont Park in Pennsylvania. It still runs today. It is the world's oldest working roller coaster.

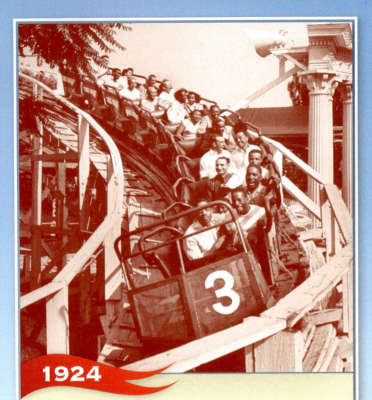

**1924**

The Bobs opens at Riverview Park in Chicago. Its cars look like bobsleds. More than 1,500 coasters are built in the 1920s. The Bobs is among the finest.

**1953**

The first major roller coaster opens in Tokyo, Japan. It is built around the edge of a park. This is one of the first roller coasters built after World War II.

**1959**

The first steel roller coaster opens at Disneyland in California. It is called the Matterhorn Bobsleds. The cars twist through a model of the Swiss mountain called the Matterhorn.

### 1977
The first shuttle roller coasters open. A shuttle coaster does not make a complete circle. The cars go forward and backward along the same track. King Kobra at Kings Dominion in Virginia is one of the first shuttle coasters.

### 1964
The Serpent of Fire in Mexico City becomes the first roller coaster to stand 30.5 meters (100 feet) tall.

### 1981
The American Eagle opens at Six Flags Great America in Gurnee, Illinois. It is one of the longest and fastest wooden roller coasters.

### 1972
The Racer opens at Kings Island in Ohio. Kings Island is a large theme park. The Racer has two tracks with a train on each one. The trains race each other. People get excited about roller coasters again.

### 1982
The first stand-up roller coaster opens in Japan. Passengers stand up during the ride.

### 1997
Skytrak Total is the first flying roller coaster. It's in Manchester, United Kingdom. Riders are facedown. They feel like they are flying.

### 1996
Flight of Fear opens at Kings Island and Kings Dominion. They are the first coasters to move cars using **magnetism.** Magnetism is a force. It pulls metal things made with iron. Magnets are in the track and under the cars. Electricity passes through the magnets. This pushes and pulls the cars.

### 2001
The first coaster that uses compressed air to push off cars opens at Kings Dominion. The HyperSonic XLC speeds up faster than any other coaster.

### 2005

Kingda Ka opens at Six Flags Great Adventure in New Jersey. This coaster has a 45-story drop.

### 2007

Maverick opens at Cedar Point in Ohio. It is the first coaster with a twisted horseshoe roll. The rider rolls over in a complete circle.

### 2009

Manta opens at SeaWorld Orlando. People ride face down and head first. They move like manta rays.

From boards on wheels, roller coasters have come a long way in 200 years. Today's coasters safely show you what it's like to rocket into space or soar like an eagle. No wonder millions of people ride roller coasters every year.

**Check In** What role does gravity play in how roller coasters work?

**GENRE** Science Article | **Read to find out** how forces make roller coasters so wild.

# WILD COASTER

by Kathleen F. Lally

Imagine these riders shrieking, screaming, and squealing. Who could blame them? They feel like they're flying! They lie facedown and swoop through the air.

The **work** of flying coasters is moving riders over a distance. A chain pulls the car up a spiral track. The riders dangle beneath the track. They reach for their handgrips. The ride is about to change.

The car swoops down from the top. Work is done as **gravity** pulls the car down. The car twists, turns, and rolls down the track. It stops less than a minute later. Now the riders know how a flying superhero feels! This ride is not as extreme as others. All strapped in? Get ready for some wild rides!

Flying Coaster, Genting, Pahang, Malaysia ▸

# Fastest

The Formula Rossa isn't an ordinary roller coaster. The cars look like Formula One race cars. You don't have to wear a helmet. You do have to wear safety goggles. You'll need them at these high speeds. They'll keep sand out of your eyes.

The Formula Rossa cars start on a flat track. You reach a speed of 240 kilometers per hour (149 miles per hour) in only 5 seconds! That gives the cars enough **energy of motion** to race up the first hill. The cars slow down as they climb. They slow because their energy of motion changes to **stored energy.** The higher the cars go, the more stored energy they have. At the top of the hill the cars have a lot of stored energy. That is because they are high above Earth.

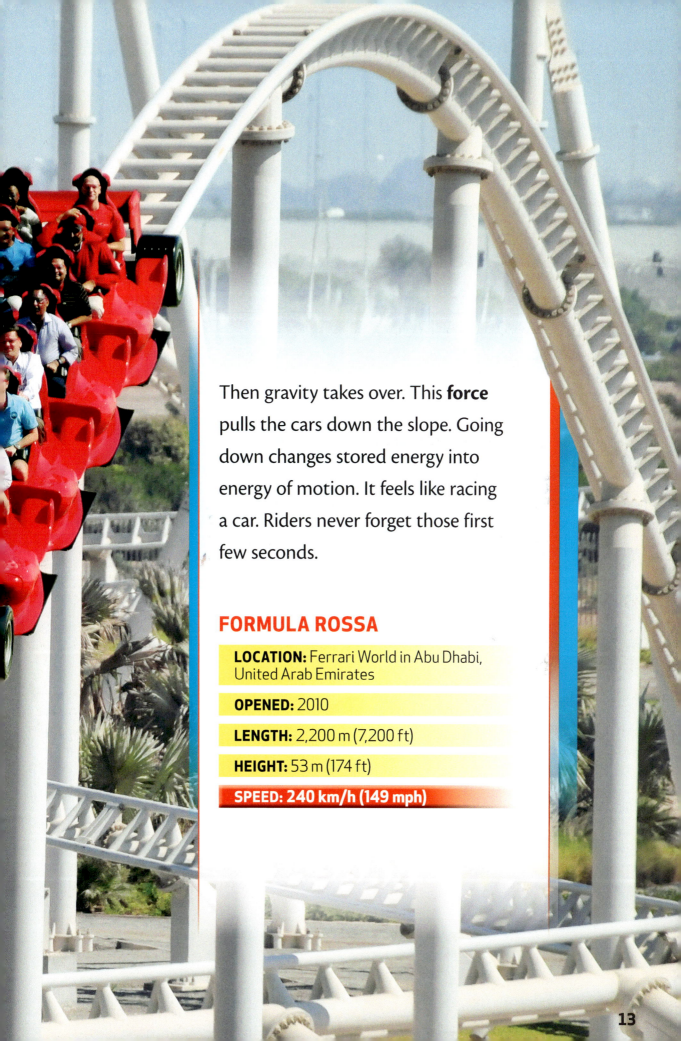

Then gravity takes over. This **force** pulls the cars down the slope. Going down changes stored energy into energy of motion. It feels like racing a car. Riders never forget those first few seconds.

### FORMULA ROSSA

**LOCATION:** Ferrari World in Abu Dhabi, United Arab Emirates

**OPENED:** 2010

**LENGTH:** 2,200 m (7,200 ft)

**HEIGHT:** 53 m (174 ft)

**SPEED:** 240 km/h (149 mph)

# HIGHEST

"Arms down, head back, and hold on!"

You're about to be launched on the Kingda Ka. The launch track is flat and straight. Then it goes straight UP! Kingda Ka is king when it comes to height!

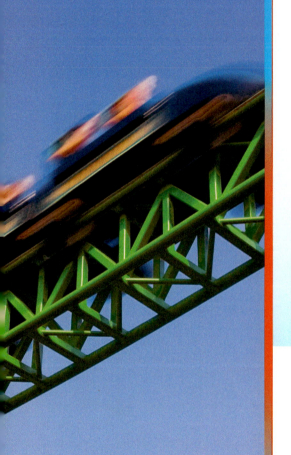

The cars reach 206 kilometers per hour (128 miles per hour) in just 3.5 seconds! The force of the launch shoots the cars up the tower. You reach a height of 139 meters (456 feet). That is a world record.

You zip up and over the top of the hill. The cars start moving down. But your body feels as though it is still moving up. You are strapped in, but you still feel a bit of "air time."

### KINGDA KA

**LOCATION:** Six Flags Great Adventure in Jackson, New Jersey, United States

**OPENED:** 2005

**LENGTH:** 950 m (3,118 ft)

**HEIGHT:** 139 m (456 ft)

**SPEED:** 206 km/h (128 mph)

# LONGEST

Most coaster rides last only about a minute. One coaster ride lasts four times as long! Buckle up for the Steel Dragon 2000.

Chains pull the cars up the hill to the top of the dragon's head. The climb lasts more than a minute. Then you swoop down the dragon's back and tail. You go a distance of three football fields. That drop gives you energy of motion.

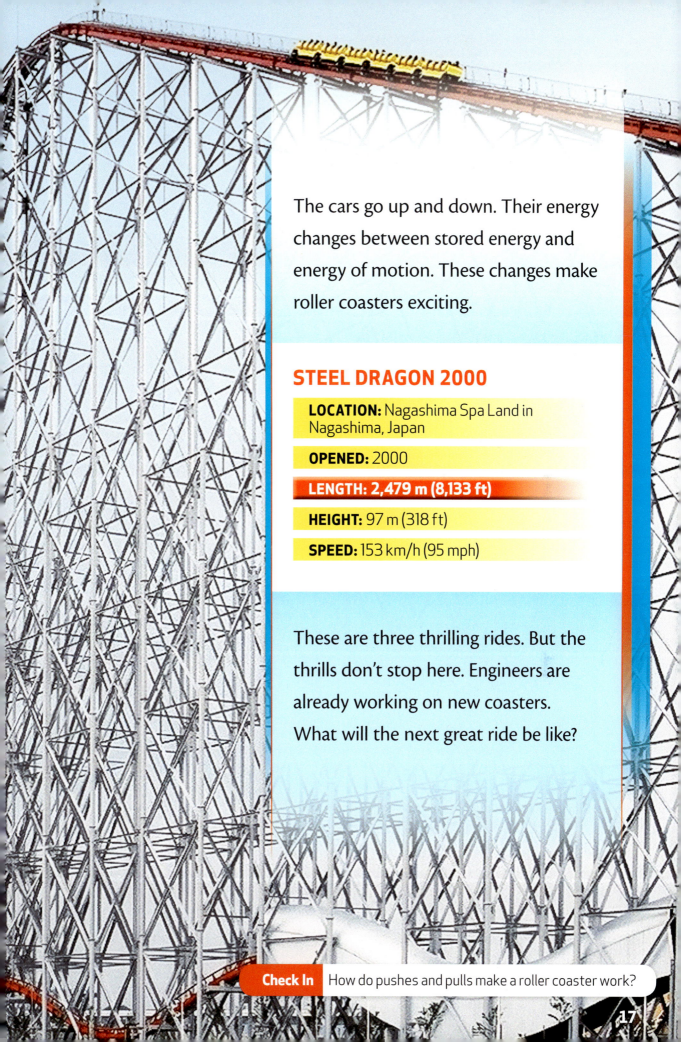

The cars go up and down. Their energy changes between stored energy and energy of motion. These changes make roller coasters exciting.

### STEEL DRAGON 2000

**LOCATION:** Nagashima Spa Land in Nagashima, Japan

**OPENED:** 2000

**LENGTH:** 2,479 m (8,133 ft)

**HEIGHT:** 97 m (318 ft)

**SPEED:** 153 km/h (95 mph)

These are three thrilling rides. But the thrills don't stop here. Engineers are already working on new coasters. What will the next great ride be like?

**Check In** How do pushes and pulls make a roller coaster work?

**GENRE** How-To Article  **Read to find out** how to design and build a model roller coaster.

# How to Make a Model Roller Coaster

by Judy Elgin Jensen

Suppose you could build a roller coaster. How would it look? What kinds of thrills would it have? Here's your chance. Build a roller coaster model! Engineers use science to solve problems. Engineers who design roller coasters build models to test their designs. Will the car stay on the tracks? Will the hills provide enough **force** to move the cars?

You can make roller coaster models out of many materials. Try the ones listed here. Then work with a partner. Follow the steps.

# Materials

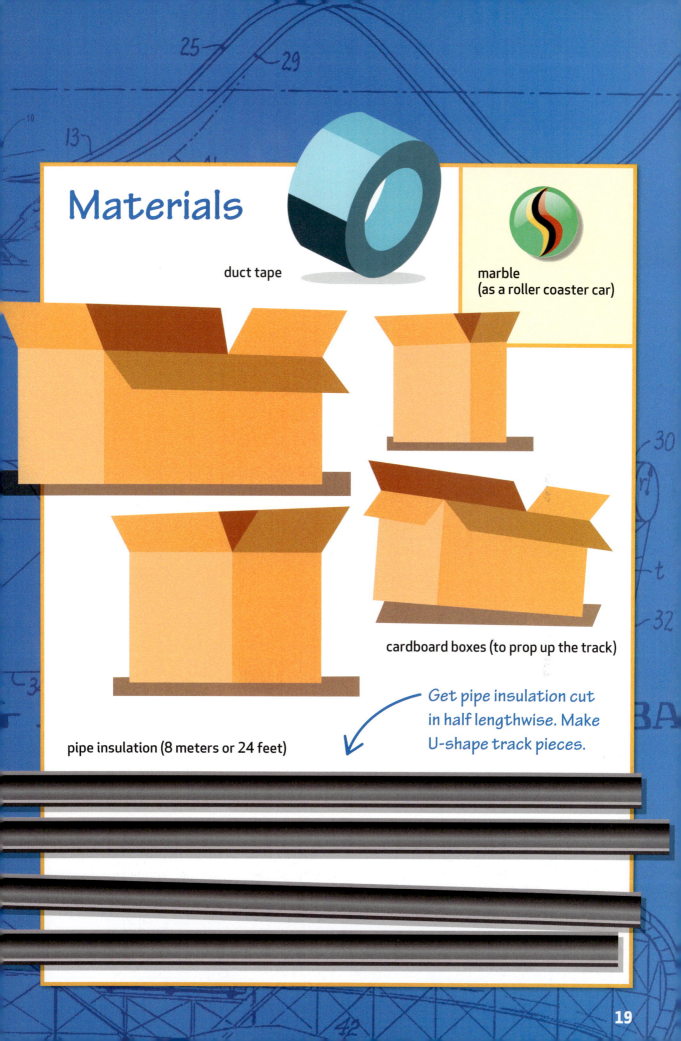

duct tape

marble (as a roller coaster car)

cardboard boxes (to prop up the track)

pipe insulation (8 meters or 24 feet)

*Get pipe insulation cut in half lengthwise. Make U-shape track pieces.*

# Step 1: Make a Plan and Sketch It

Think about what features you want your roller coaster to have. Do you want more than one hill? Do you want bends, loops, or twists?

Draw your roller coaster. The lift hill must be high enough. It must give your coaster car enough energy to roll through the whole course. Your car will be a marble. But the marble can't roll too fast. If it flies off the track, the real coaster would be dangerous.

# Step 2: Build Your Design

Build your model. Start with the lift hill. Connect the pieces of pipe insulation with duct tape. Tape the track to boxes, chairs, and tables. Follow your sketch. But if you see a better way to do something, go for it!

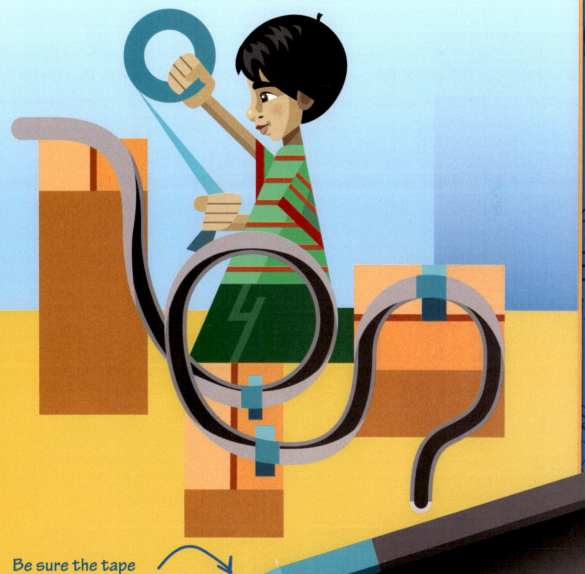

Be sure the tape won't block the rolling marble.

# Step 3: Test and Improve Your Model

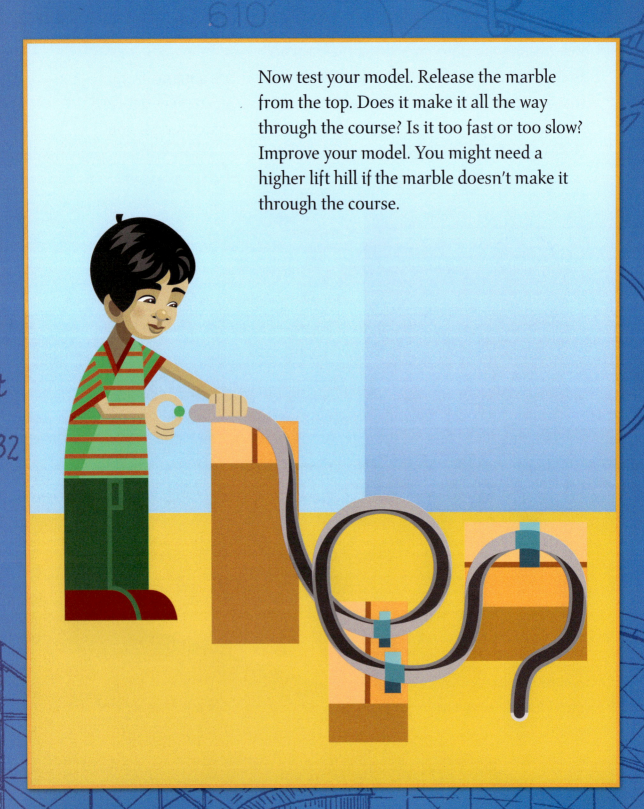

Now test your model. Release the marble from the top. Does it make it all the way through the course? Is it too fast or too slow? Improve your model. You might need a higher lift hill if the marble doesn't make it through the course.

# Step 4: Share Your Results

Show your model to your friends and family. Give it a name. Demonstrate it at a science fair. Explain how the marble's energy changes between **stored energy** and **energy of motion.** Compare and contrast your model with your classmates' coasters.

Create a name. It should tell your coaster's coolest feature.

SAMUEL'S SNAKEY SPIRAL

What's next? Work with others to create the tallest, hilliest, or loopiest coaster! You might need other materials. You already know about the cars changing energy. Now just be creative and have fun!

**Check In** How might you adjust your model if the marble keeps flying off the track?

## Discuss

1. What connections can you make among the three pieces in *Roller Coasters*?

2. Cite evidence from "The History of Roller Coasters" to describe how coaster design changed over time.

3. How did you use what you learned in "The History of Roller Coasters" and "Wild Coasters" to design your own?

4. Compare and contrast energy of motion and stored energy in two roller coasters from this book.

5. What do you still wonder about roller coaster design? What would be some good ways to find more information?